D1505795

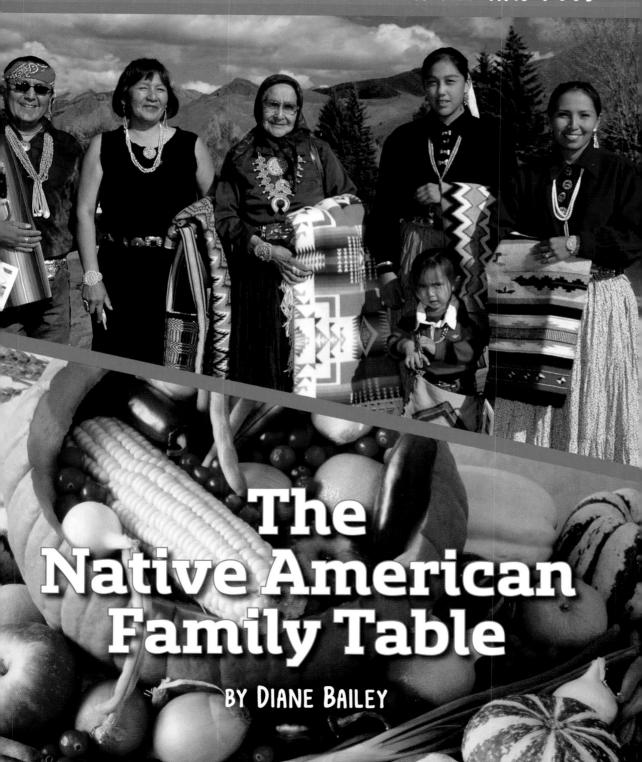

CONNECTING CULTURES THROUGH FAMILY AND FOOD

The Native American Family Table

BY DIANE BAILEY

Connecting Cultures Through Family and Food

The African Family Table

The Chinese Family Table

The Greek Family Table

The Indian Family Table

The Italian Family Table

The Japanese Family Table

The Mexican Family Table

The Middle Eastern Family Table

The Native American Family Table

The South American Family Table

The Thai Family Table

CONNECTING CULTURES THROUGH FAMILY AND FOOD

The Native American Family Table

By Diane Bailey

MASON CREST

Mason Crest
450 Parkway Drive, Suite D
Broomall, PA 19008
www.masoncrest.com

© 2019 by Mason Crest, an imprint of National Highlights, Inc.

Printed and bound in the United States of America.

First printing
9 8 7 6 5 4 3 2 1

Series ISBN: 978-1-4222-4041-0
Hardback ISBN: 978-1-4222-4050-2
EBook ISBN: 978-1-4222-7748-5

Produced by Shoreline Publishing Group LLC
Santa Barbara, California
Editorial Director: James Buckley Jr.
Designer: Tom Carling
Production: Patty Kelley
www.shorelinepublishing.com
Front cover: NativeStock.com/Angel Wynn (top); Dreamstime.com/Janice Hazeldine (bottom)

Library of Congress Cataloging-in-Publication Data on file with the Publisher

Contents

KEY ICONS TO LOOK FOR

Words to Understand: These words with their easy-to-understand definitions will increase the reader's understanding of the text, while building vocabulary skills.

Sidebars: This boxed material within the main text allows readers to build knowledge, gain insights, explore possibilities, and broaden their perspectives by weaving together additional information to provide realistic and holistic perspectives.

Educational Videos: Readers can view videos by scanning our QR codes, providing them with additional educational content to supplement the text. Examples include news coverage, moments in history, speeches, iconic moments, and much more!

Text-Dependent Questions: These questions send the reader back to the text for more careful attention to the evidence presented here.

Research Projects: Readers are pointed toward areas of further inquiry connected to each chapter. Suggestions are provided for projects that encourage deeper research and analysis.

Series Glossary of Key Terms: This back-of-the-book glossary contains terminology used throughout this series. Words found here increase the reader's ability to read and comprehend higher-level books and articles in this field.

Introduction

A Choctaw legend tells of two men who go out on a hunting trip. As night falls and darkness comes, they stop to make camp and start a fire. They have very little food, however, just a single rabbit to share between them. They cook the rabbit, but before they can eat their meager meal, they hear the sound of crying. Upon going to investigate, they find a woman all alone. She tells them that she has gotten lost and is hungry. Wanting to help, the hunters take her to their camp. Despite their own hunger, they offer her the rabbit, but the woman takes just one bite. Then she thanks them, and tells them to return the next day to where they had found her. With that, she is gone.

 Naming Rights

Several terms have been used to describe the people who first lived in the Americas, including American Indian and Native American. Some dislike these terms though, because the word "America" originated with Europeans, and Native people had been here long before the Europeans arrived. For that reason, some prefer to be called indigenous peoples or, in Canada, people of First Nations. The title of this book uses "Native American" to most clearly refer both to the region now called North America, as well as to the people who first populated it. Throughout the text, however, a number of terms are used to recognize the diversity and different opinions within the Native community.

Following the woman's instructions, the next day the hunters return to the spot. She is not there, but in her place they find a strange, tall plant with silken tassels at the top. They pluck one of the plant's fruits, peel back the green coating, and find a cob lined with rows of small, seed-like kernels. When the hunters return home, they plant the kernels, and soon new plants grow. It turns out the woman was the daughter of Sun Father and Moon Mother. To reward the hunters for their kindness, she had given them and their people the gift of corn.

Food is tied to culture, religion, family, community, and more in Native American nations.

Probably no other food is as important to the Native American story than corn, but it's also just one food in an incredibly varied cuisine. In fact, more than half of the foods eaten around the world originated in the Americas. Today, the ideas of American dining—particularly in the United States—come largely from the influence of immigrants. What did the Italians bring? The Irish? The German? But it's the people who were here first, the Native Americans, who provided the true foundation of American cuisine. The story of Native American food is one of creativity, tenacity, and incredible diversity.

1

An Ancient Culture

The traffic on the bridge wasn't heavy, but it was steady. A few people one day, maybe a few dozen a month after that—no one knows for sure, because it happened between 12,000 and 15,000 years ago, during the Pleistocene Epoch, commonly called the Ice Age.

During this time, the Earth's temperatures were cooler, and much of the Earth's water was locked up in ice, lowering sea levels by hundreds of feet. A land bridge—called Beringia—formed in the far north, between what are now Russia, Canada, and the US state of Alaska.

Words to Understand

domesticate   to tame or control wild animals or plants

foodways   the social, cultural, and economic aspects of food and dining

foraging   finding food in the wild

indigenous   original or native to a particular place or area

sustenance   food that keeps people alive

yields   in agriculture, the food that is successfully harvested

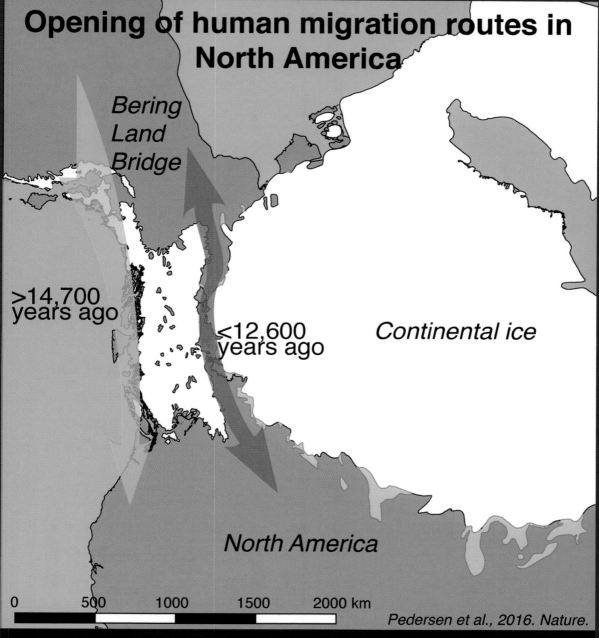

Opening of human migration routes in North America

Bering Land Bridge

>14,700 years ago

<12,600 years ago

Continental ice

North America

| 0 | 500 | 1000 | 1500 | 2000 km |

Pedersen et al., 2016. Nature.

Scientists say that humans came to what is now North America over a now-submerged land bridge from Asia through Alaska.

9

Over that bridge came peoples from Asia, perhaps a few thousand in total. (Some evidence shows that humans may have arrived much earlier, some 40,000 to 60,000 years ago, but a large wave came during the Pleistocene.) Then, by about 11,000 years ago, global temperatures began to warm again. Ice melted, sea levels rose, and the Beringia land bridge was covered by water. Once again, Asia and the Americas were separated. The people who had arrived, though, had established themselves. They spread to the east across modern-day Canada, and then south over what is now the United States, and Central and South America.

Regional Flair

Hundreds of tribes have lived in the vast area of the Americas, and they all superbly adapted to their particular regions. Whether their environment was hot or cold, wet or dry, lush with vegetation or seemingly barren, their **foodways** developed to take advantage of everything nature had to offer.

In North America, for example, cultures in the Pacific Northwest had a diet that depended heavily on fish, particularly salmon, that ran in the northern rivers. The Plains Indians, meanwhile, might have eaten occasional fish from midcontinental rivers. However, they relied mainly on land animals, notably buffalo, which ranged the central plains in massive herds.

In other areas, Native Americans ate fowl such as goose, duck, pheasant, and turkey, as well as small game such as opossums and raccoons. Snakes, turtles, and insects were also plentiful food sources. Valuable calories came from fat in sources like bear backs and beaver tails.

Plant foods were also widely consumed. Corn, potatoes, beans, squash, acorns, rice, onions, and celery, and all kinds of fruit were staples of many Indian tribes. Everybody has heard of blueberries, strawberries, and blackberries, but those were just a few of dozens of berry species available in North America. And although many people associate potatoes with Ireland, they are in fact **indigenous** to the Western hemisphere. In Peru, ancient cultures cultivated some three thousand different varieties of potatoes!

This mural in Olympia, Washington, shows Pacific Northwest Native Americans in traditional canoes, sometimes used for fishing.

Many Native tribes were migratory. Rather than living permanently in one place, they traveled around according to the seasons, following the food sources. Sometimes they moved to be nearby when grapes ripened. Sometimes it was to follow a roaming herd of buffalo. Over time, many indigenous people incorporated organized agriculture into their societies. They learned to **domesticate** plants to better control when and where they grew, and to maximize their **yields**. In more temperate climates, people might only plant enough to feed themselves for the season. In colder zones farther north, however, they might plant large

Rich Navajo farmland like this in Canyon de Chelly Park in Arizona has been cultivated for centuries.

amounts of crops, more than they could eat in a single year. They knew that they could lose everything to an early frost. By saving extra food in productive years, they could get safely through lean times.

Trade Routes

Despite strong regional cultures, Native American tribes were far from isolated. A network of trade routes stretched throughout the Americas, creating sophisticated connections among people. In North America, farming tribes in what is now North Dakota and Ontario, Canada, traded corn, squash, and beans for the meat and furs of animals brought in by hunters farther north. In the Sonoran Desert—which stretches across lands that are now the southwestern United States and northern Mexico—the Papago collected salt that they traded for pumpkin seeds with the Mohave people, who lived farther north in what became California.

Puebloans in northwestern New Mexico founded a trade system that

Ancient farming techniques

was based on turquoise. That blue-green stone, mined from area canyons, was used in jewelry and other decorative objects, and acquired spiritual significance. In hard times, it was a reliable currency to trade for food or other basic necessities.

Trading wasn't limited just to objects. The Hohokam people, who lived in Arizona, were skilled farmers. To cope with the dry deserts of the southwest, they developed sophisticated irrigation systems. They then shared this technology with other cultures, helping the spread of agriculture.

The Hohokam people used innovative farming techniques, including small dams to harness the available water in the desert.

Ties to the Earth

Acommon thread emerges among almost all Native cultures: Food was not viewed simply as **sustenance**, something necessary to continue from one day to the next. Instead, most Native Americans formed intimate relationships with the Earth and the plants and animals it supported. They believed that nature's gifts should only be accepted with the proper gratitude and reverence. Every aspect of acquiring, raising, preparing, and eating food came with rituals. When hunters made a kill, they offered back a part of the animal in thanks. Farmers offered prayers to the spirits

 ## The Three Sisters

Corn, beans, and squash were three pillars of the Native American diet. They were hardy, widespread, nutritious, and relatively easy to grow. Farmers know that certain plants complement each other, and that growing them together can increase the odds of success. Ancient Native Americans discovered that the "three sisters" of corn, beans, and squash all benefited from each other. Tall corn stalks provided natural poles for bean vines to climb. The stalks gave shade to squash plants. The beans put nitrogen into the soil, which was essential for all three plants. And the leaves of squash plants shielded the soil from the sun to help retain moisture and discourage weeds from sprouting.

to ensure good crops. Sacred ceremonies accompanied harvest feasts. In the Hidatsa tribe of present-day North Dakota, young women kept watch over the corn to make sure the birds did not eat it. In the book Buffalo Bird Woman's Garden, a Hidatsa woman born about 1839 recalls a tradition that likely had persisted for centuries. "We cared for our corn in those days as we could care for a child," she told an interviewer in the early 1900s. "We thought that our growing corn liked to hear us sing, just as children like to hear their mother sing to them."

Food dictated not only where people lived and what they ate, but how they structured their societies. Men in the ancient Clovis culture, who

Corn has played a central role in several Native American tribal cultures, both as a key food ingredient and also as part of harvest cermonies.

Settling the Score

The game of lacrosse has its roots in an ancient Indian game known as stickball. (An early Iroquois name for the game was *baggataway*. Its modern name comes from French; the sticks used reminded settlers from France of those used by their bishops, a stick called *la crosse*.) Not only was it a test of skill and athleticism, it was also a way to resolve disputes. In ancient times, games and sports were frequently used as alternatives to fighting. By channeling their grievances into the controlled setting of a relatively peaceful game, people hoped to avoid the more violent prospect of war.

To prepare for the stickball "battle," players often followed a strict diet to help their chances of winning. They would fast directly before the match, and before that they would avoid certain foods. Frogs were out, because they were believed to make players more likely to suffer from broken bones. Rabbits were also on the blacklist—no player wanted to behave like a scared, confused rabbit when bravery and skill were necessary for success.

lived about 9,000 BCE, passed down specialized hunting knowledge from one generation to the next. Such knowledge was critical for the society to survive, so when the Clovis people married, it was the woman who was expected to leave her family and join that of her husband's. Although Clovis women contributed to the food needs of the community by gathering roots, berries, and other wild plants, it was believed that these skills were secondary and portable. Thus, it made sense for women to go with their husbands, rather than the other way around. In some cultures the opposite held true. **Foraging** knowledge could be extremely localized, so it was not desirable for women to leave areas that they understood well.

Arrowheads and decorative objects are most of what remains from the wide-ranging Clovis cultures of North and Central America.

No matter what the specific routine or habit was, the underlying purpose was to ensure that everyone had enough food. It was an approach that worked for centuries. But beginning in the late 15th century, the traditional ways of Native Americans were severely tested.

Text-Dependent Questions:

1. Why did people in cold climates often plant large amounts of crops?

2. What foods make up the "three sisters"?

3. What did the Hidatsa people do to help their corn grow?

Research Project:

Find out what Native American tribes live or lived in the area where you live. Make a list of what foods they ate, and the ingredients of certain dishes. Which foods are readily available today, and what would be difficult to find?

SMALL MEALS

Any of the three staples of the Native diet—or the three sisters—makes a good base for a classic appetizer: a fritter. These fried cakes or balls are simple to prepare. A cook starts with mashed corn, potatoes, or squash, and then adds any number of other ingredients to make the fritters as straightforward or elaborate as desired.

Corn fritters can get a bite from jalapeño or other chili peppers, which are native to southern climates in the Americas, or they might take on a coastal flavor with clams from the Northeast. A potato fritter can be served with a spicy peanut sauce, using two foods that are some of the oldest cultivated in the Western Hemisphere.

Cold salads, using the best of whatever's fresh in the garden, is a mainstay in Western meals; Americans tend to have a salad before the main course, while Europeans may wait until after. In Native society, however, the ingredients of salad were typically worked into the main meal, being served as condiments and relishes. Tortillas, for example, could be topped with avocados mashed into guacamole, or with a tomato or tomatillo salsa kicked into high gear with onions and peppers.

Perhaps craving a bite before the tomatoes ripened in August, or hoping to make the most of a harvest that was cut short by a cold snap, Native Americans did not just eat red tomatoes, but green ones, too. Breaded in cornmeal and fried in corn oil, their sour taste offered a varied flavor from the usual sweetness.

2

Under Threat

The close relationship indigenous peoples had with the Earth did not mean that their lifestyles were primitive or simplistic. They had a deep understanding of the natural environment, and their priorities were to take care of the land, the water, and one another. Food was central to all of this. Native Americans developed effective systems for hunting, growing, and preparing food, and every member of a community had a role.

In ancient Clovis society, sharing food was vital. It did not matter who had killed the bison, or planted the corn, or collected the pine nuts. Everyone—young,

Words to Understand

coincided happened at the same time

exceptionalism a belief that one people or culture is, by its very nature, better or superior than all others

exploitation immorally and illegally taking goods, land, or culture

immunity the ability of a human body not to become infected with a disease

22

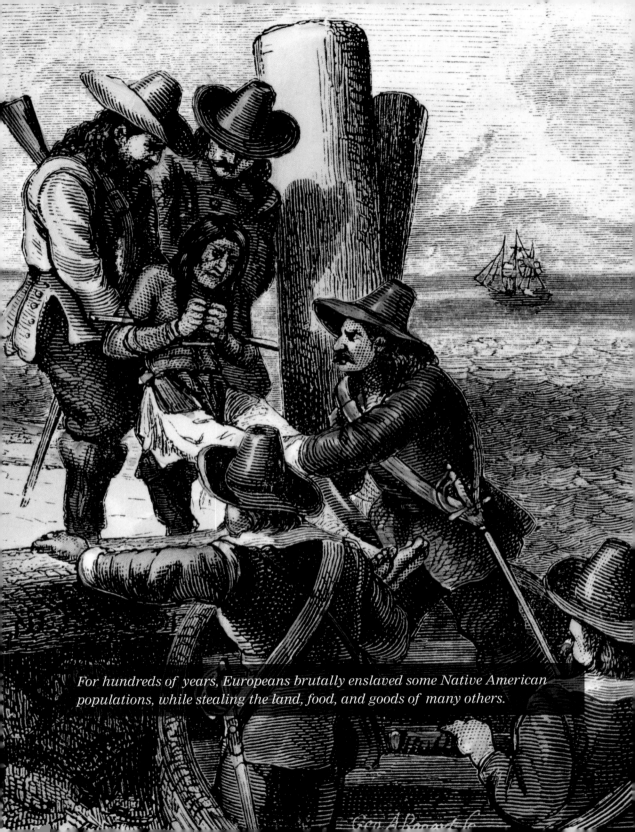

For hundreds of years, Europeans brutally enslaved some Native American populations, while stealing the land, food, and goods of many others.

old, sick, or well—shared in the bounty. People who tried to keep food for themselves were shunned. In some cases, that was even considered a criminal offense. However, when European settlers arrived, Native Americans discovered that not everyone shared their viewpoint.

Ships from Europe

Christopher Columbus was not the first European to set foot in the Americas, but he is undoubtedly the most famous. In 1492, when Columbus landed on what is the now the island of San Salvador in the Bahamas, he set off a movement of exploration and immigration—and some would say **exploitation**—that continued for centuries.

This is a replica of the surprisingly small ships, known as caravels, that Columbus used on his journeys in the 1400s.

Columbus's story is well known. He sailed from Spain (he was Italian but his voyage was paid for by the Spanish monarchy) looking for Asia. Inadvertently, he ended up on the other side of the Atlantic Ocean. Unaware that he was rather dramatically off course, he assumed he had reached India and called the native peoples he saw "Indians." Undeterred by his error, Columbus made several follow-up journeys to the New World (which was, of course, only "new" to the Europeans), and his trips sparked interest among more European explorers in the following decades. The Spanish took over much of Central and South America. The British arrived in North America in the 1600s. People also came from France, the Netherlands, and other countries.

These explorations **coincided** with the Renaissance in Europe, a time when culture and science flourished. Europeans responded with pride and self-confidence that sometimes turned into arrogance. They adopted attitudes of **exceptionalism** and entitlement. These outlooks—not to mention the Europeans' more powerful weapons—eclipsed the views of Native Americans.

Europeans valued capitalist, individualistic approaches. These directly clashed with Native Americans, who tended to think the opposite way—placing the benefit for many over the advantage for a few. What many Europeans *did* recognize was the Indians' superior skills in dealing with their environment. James Adair, an Irish settler who traveled to the Americas in the 1700s, wrote, "If an Indian were driven out into the extensive woods with only a knife and a tomahawk, or small hatchet, it is not to be doubted but he would fatten, even if a wolf would starve."

Early settlers certainly benefited from the knowledge of the people they found in these "new" lands, people who often shared their food with the settlers and taught them how to grow their own. There are records of several harvest or "Thanksgiving" feasts shared by British settlers and Indians along the East Coast. But ultimately the settlers proved ungracious, demanding more and more food. If the Indians refused, the British sometimes burned the Indians' homes and stole food. Before long, Native Americans realized Europeans did not share their vision of caring for each other and using resources wisely.

In 1622, Powhatan Indians clashed with Jamestown, Virginia, settlers who attempted to take their land and force them to change to European

The English settlement of Jamestown, Virginia, has been recreated and is now a place where people can learn about life in early colonial days.

A Leg Up

The first Native Americans shared the continent with the ancient relatives of horses. But horses became extinct in the Americas about 8,000 years ago—possibly due to climate change—leaving humans without one of their food sources. It was only in the 1500s that horses returned, brought back to Central America by Spanish explorers and settlers. These horses eventually spread into North America and were domesticated by Native American tribes. Rather than being a food source, however, horses became companions and tools in hunting. Riding a horse was faster (and much less tiring) when it came to chasing buffalo herds, and they greatly increased the range that hunters could travel. Scientists have found that once horses were introduced, some tribes switched from a sedentary, agricultural lifestyle to one that relied more on nomadic hunting—a change made in part because European settlers made it impossible for American Indians to stay in their homelands.

lifestyles. The Powhatan attacked the settlers, killing many. In some cases, they stuffed bread or dirt into the mouths of the dead, a message that the settlers were greedy and wasteful. To this day, the American holiday of Thanksgiving brings up bitter feelings among many Native Americans.

Changing Foodways

European settlement spread with devastating results to indigenous peoples. Millions were killed in wars or died from European diseases such as smallpox, to which they had no **immunity**. Millions more were forced from their ancestral lands, driven into smaller areas and into geographical regions that held no history or familiarity for them.

In California, Spanish missionaries built fences around their settlements, blocking Native Americans from getting to their traditional foraging sites. Meanwhile, the Spaniards' hogs gorged themselves on

Father Serra controversy in California

acorns—a primary food source for the Indians—and their cattle grazed their way across acres of countryside, creating too much competition for the area's natural resources.

In Canada, the growing fur trade fundamentally changed First Nations' foodways. European traders enlisted First Nations hunters to bring in seals, foxes, and other animals whose furs were prized in European markets. Over-hunting put a huge strain on these animals, threatening a food source that indigenous peoples had always depended on. At the same time, Europeans traded to these communities unfamiliar foods that were less nutritious. Particularly deadly was the introduction of alcohol.

First Nations tribes in Canada took part in the fur trade with Europeans.

Farther to the south, the range of massive bison herds became cramped as Europeans took land for farms and ranches. Railroad tracks cut sprawling habitats into smaller and smaller pieces. Worst of all was commercial hunting. Although American Indians killed buffalo for food and pelts, it was only a small fraction of what Europeans took. By some estimates, European hunters killed thousands of animals every day. The tremendous loss of animals destroyed the lifestyle of Plains Indians, and nearly drove the buffalo to extinction.

Those who did stay on their lands struggled to grow the strange crops that Europeans introduced. Buffalo Bird Woman remembered, "We Hidatsas did not like potatoes, because they smelled so strongly! Then we sometimes dug up our potatoes and took them into our earth lodges; and when cold weather came, the potatoes were frozen, and spoiled. For these reasons we did not take much interest in our potatoes, and often left them in the ground."

Reservations

The European hunger to acquire land in the Americas proved to be too powerful a force for Native tribes to resist. Native Americans were pushed into smaller spaces, often far from their traditional homes. Beginning in the 1830s, tens of thousands of Choctaw, Cherokee, Creek, and other American Indians were forced to walk from their homes in the Southeastern United States—a region white settlers had decided was desirable—to emptier lands west of the Mississippi River. Thousands died on this Trail of Tears. In the 1860s, thousands of Diné (Navajo) were forced to take the Long Walk, a trek of 300 miles across New Mexico, to a reservation at Fort Sumner that was far too small to accommodate them

Peaches and Sheep

Hundreds of fruits are native to the Americas, but peaches are not one of them. And of the many four-legged creatures that roam the Western Hemisphere, sheep were not among the original inhabitants. Both peaches and sheep were introduced by Europeans centuries ago, but they have become important parts of Native culture.

Spanish missionaries did not have much luck growing peaches in the warm climates of Central and South America, but they flourished in the cooler temperatures of northern Mexico and the southern United States. The crop spread to American Indians. Tribes from Florida to California soon starting planting their own orchards—and many still do. Spanish conquistadors also brought sheep to the Americas, where Natives—especially the Diné—adopted them into their culture. The *churro* is a small breed of sheep that Diné ranchers have raised for centuries, both for food and for its wool.

all. These events are well known in the history of Native Americans, but they are just a couple of examples.

The US and Canadian governments signed treaties with indigenous tribes, promising them access to at least a portion of their native lands. However, these governments then went on to violate many of the treaties, making it impossible to sustain traditional lifestyles.

By the close of the 19th century, the picture of Native American life that was common a few centuries earlier had virtually disappeared. Millions had died. They were smaller in number and smaller in stature due to disease and malnutrition. They were separated from their

In the late 1800s and early 1900s, the US government forced many Native Americans into "assimilation" schools like this one in South Dakota.

traditional homelands and sometimes from their families. They were severely damaged, but they were not broken.

Memories lived, and traditions lay dormant, but not extinguished. Over the next century, Native Americans would work to reclaim their rightful place.

Text-Dependent Questions:

1. How did the introduction of horses change Native American lifestyles?

2. What is one way that Spanish missionaries made life more difficult for American Indians living in California?

3. What was the Long Walk?

Research Project:

Look into some of the written accounts early settlers recorded about their observations of Native Americans. What was positive? Negative? How do you think these reports would be received today?

SOME BASICS

Wheat—and the flour made from it—only came to the Americas with the arrival of European settlers, but other types of bread were widespread in the Native diet.

Cornbread, of course, was popular. Breads were also made from ground cattails, nuts, amaranth, cassava (tapioca), or the pods from mesquite trees. In the western United States, Native peoples ground acorns into a powder, then put it in bags and flushed it with water to rinse out the bitter taste before baking it into bread. Adding honey, maple sap, or berries gave breads a sweet flavor, while unsweetened breads might be served with meat or fish.

Perhaps no other food is as closely associated with the Native diet as pemmican. The recipe is simple: dried meat, or jerky, often from deer or buffalo, was pounded into a powder, and mixed with berries. Melted animal fat was stirred in to make everything stick together, and the result was stored in leather bags. Pemmican was a lightweight, protein-rich food that could last for years. It was ideal for hunters to pack on a long trip, and, if necessary, could sustain entire communities during lean winters.

Probably the most popular beverage for Native Americans was just plain water, but they also enjoyed juices made from berries. They also drank herbal teas brewed from the leaves or roots of plants such as mint, ginseng, and sassafras; the flowers from hibiscus; or the bark from elm trees. In Central America, people enjoyed the flavor of cacao beans, which were brewed into a strong, hot drink flavored with other native plants, including chili peppers and vanilla. Europeans eventually added sugar to the cacao drink to make a closer version of what we now know as hot chocolate.

3

Reconnecting

The day's work starts at sunrise. That's when the Osage in northern Oklahoma go to the fields to pick corn, shuck and silk it, and then boil it for a few minutes to "set the milk." Then the cobs are tossed onto a pile of husks to cool. "It's a pretty sight, early morning in July," says Raymond Red Corn, the assistant chief of the Osage Nation. Next, everyone sits in a circle with a sheet spread between them, and uses a spoon to pop the whole kernels off the cobs. Then it's all laid out to dry for the afternoon. After several hours, they grab the edges of the sheet and shake it. "When it rattles, it's done," says Red Corn. "That will preserve corn for a full year. All you have to do is rehydrate it in the soup."

Words to Understand

assimilate become part of a different society, country, or group

genetically modified changed on the deepest chemical level from the original

obesity being grossly overweight

powwow name for a celebration or gathering of Native American people

3 6

For the Osage Nation, red corn is a part of important rituals that its members use to bind generations and continue ancient traditions.

Red Corn's family has raised this particular variety of red corn, and prepared it this particular way, for centuries. "These traditions were passed down through my family as traditional food preservation techniques," he says, but it takes effort to keep them alive in a modern world. "They're not lost, but they're sure rusty."

Nurturing Traditions

In the 1900s and 2000s, as backyard gardens were replaced by government stores on reservations, it became a struggle to maintain ancient traditions. For centuries, many Native tribes had celebrated the hunt, or the planting and harvesting of crops with a ceremony or festival. The Green Corn Festival, for example, occurred when the corn first began to ripen. A proper ceremony would guarantee that the rest of the crop would be successful. Other festivals gave thanks for maple sugar in the spring, or the first strawberries in summer. The *Powamuya* ceremony among the Hopi was a time to plant bean sprouts to ensure a good harvest later on. In the Pacific Northwest, the First Foods festival was held annually at the winter solstice, when the salmon of the northwestern rivers began to run. According to tribal legends, salmon were the first food available to indigenous peoples. (Deer came second, and *sliiton*, a type of bitterroot, followed next.)

Unfortunately, white settlers typically viewed Native Americans and their lifestyles as being substandard to those of Europeans. They attempted to **assimilate** Native Americans into a white culture, dictating what indigenous people should wear, how they should talk (their native languages were prohibited), or how they should celebrate their culture. In practice, this often meant not celebrating it at all. Europeans reasoned that if Indians were permitted to follow their traditional ways, they would resist assimilation, so they often banned **powwows**, festivals, or other Native practices outright.

It would take more than a white man's law to crush centuries of traditions, though. Powwows—with their dancing, singing, and cooking—moved indoors, into structures with no windows to the outside. Celebrations perhaps became quieter, but they were not forgotten. Eventually, laws were reversed, powwows were permitted again, and Native Americans could practice their traditions without fear of punishment.

Formal ceremonies and festivals are just one facet of a much larger Native culture, but they do serve to highlight traditional beliefs and

The traditional celebration of a powwow, as here in Idaho at the annual Julyamsh Pow Wow, brings together groups of Native American nations.

practices, and food is at the forefront. "What our elders tell us over and over and over is that everything revolves around food; everything revolves around meals," says Red Corn. "Food is always part of it, but there isn't just some 'food ceremony'," he explains. "It's far too integrated."

In addition, techniques can vary, and traditions can change. "You will never hear an Osage say, 'This is the way you make corn soup.' You will hear them say, 'This is the way my grandmother taught me to make it,'" he says. "No one person's way is held out as better than some other person's. It's all okay."

Health Matters

When Europeans first arrived in the Americas, they noticed the excellent health of indigenous people. They were tall and muscular. They stood straight, with no signs of bone decay or arthritis. Their teeth weren't rotted. (Unlike many Europeans, most Native Americans still had their teeth.) They didn't get sick very much, and their strength and stamina were remarkable. In the words of Spanish explorer Cabeza de Vaca, "The men could run after a deer for an entire day without resting and without apparent fatigue."

By the 19th century this picture had worsened dramatically. The US and Canadian governments had forced Native Americans to live on reservations. Denied access to their traditional food sources, Native Americans were forced to eat bulk rations provided by the government. They got a lot of sugar, white flour, and lard—cheap food with a long shelf life. There was salmon from cans and breakfast cereal from boxes. Chef Sean Sherman is an Oglala-Lakota who grew up in the 1970s and 1980s on the Pine Ridge reservation in South Dakota. During his childhood, "A lot of what we ate was an echo of what the foods had been," he recalled in a 2016 interview. "With the amount of oppression that happened on Pine Ridge, a lot of the food systems had been pretty successfully wiped away."

This steady diet of processed food was high in calories and relatively low in nutrients. Rates of **obesity**, diabetes, and heart disease soared among the Native population. The connection was obvious, but it was a hard pattern to break. John Fire Lame Deer, a Mineconju-Lakota Sioux who died in 1976, grew up on a reservation. He saw first-hand the differences between Native and white diets. In a 1972 interview, he said, "In the old days we used to eat the guts out of the buffalo, making a contest of it,

This image from Pine Ridge in the 1950s illustrates the extreme poverty that many Native American nations suffered in that era; in some places, it has not improved.

The Debate Over Fry Bread

At its absolute simplest, fry bread has three ingredients: white flour, lard, and water. Some versions substitute milk for the water, and salt and sugar are common additions. But this simple food has a controversial history. When the Diné people were forcibly relocated to a reservation in eastern New Mexico, the US government supplied them with limited choices of food. Fry bread was born of necessity, from what little was available. "Fry bread was a gift of Western civilization from the days when Native people were removed from... real food," writes Suzan Shown Harjo, a Cheyenne and Muscogee Indian. "[It] is emblematic of the long trails from home and freedom to confinement and rations."

Fry bread represents a tragic point in Native history, but to some, it's also a food that symbolizes strength and perseverance in the face of oppression. It spread from the Diné to other tribes, and now is something that connects indigenous people across tribes. "Fry bread is the story of our survival," says Sherman Alexie, a writer and filmmaker with Spokane-Coeur d'Alene heritage.

People line up to buy it at powwows, and cooks compete to make the best version. Matt Chandra and Ben Jacobs operate a Native American restaurant in Denver, Colorado. They cooked fry bread at a competition, using a recipe from Jacobs' grandmother. "All the elder women came looking for us," Jacobs remembered in a 2010 interview, saying, "'Where are the boys who can cook fry bread? I didn't know boys could cook fry bread!'" Now, they see it as a way to bring Native Americans together, and to introduce Native foods to non-Natives. At their restaurant, they use it as a base for several dishes. "Fry bread is an easy introduction," says Chandra. "It's universal."

two fellows getting hold of a long piece of intestines from opposite ends, starting chewing toward the middle, seeing who can get there first; that's eating. Those buffalo guts, full of half-fermented, half-digested grass and herbs, you didn't need any pills and vitamins when you swallowed those. . . . That was food, that had the power. Not the stuff you give us today: powdered milk, dehydrated eggs, pasteurized butter, chickens that are all drumsticks or all breast; there's no bird left there."

Back to Basics

By the end of the 20th century, the direct and sometimes violent oppression by people of European descent had faded, but the destruction of Native foodways had long-term consequences. In general, physical health was markedly worse among the Native population. And Native Americans were often demoralized, since Europeans had systematically dismantled their lifestyle.

Fighting Native American obesity

Slowly, however, there was a movement to restore indigenous diets, including more fresh vegetables and fruit, whole grains, less sugar, and an emphasis on fresh, rather than processed, food.

On the surface, it's a straightforward approach, but it is by no means easy. For one thing, many Native people no longer have access to their native lands. In some places, they have been legally barred from the right to hunt, fish, or forage on their ancestral lands, or can do so only in small amounts or at certain times.

And there are still clashes with a white, commercialized society. **Genetically modified** crops and hybrid varieties are becoming staples of

Native villagers in Guatemala use traditional communal farming methods to work together to grow the food they need.

commercial farms. These foods can be easier to grow, resistant to disease, and provide higher yields. However, they can also clash with Native ways of growing food. The American dependency on monoculture—growing vast amounts of only a few types of crops—pushes out foods that aren't as widespread or hardy, and diversity is lost.

As Native Americans work to revive their foodways, a big part involves revitalizing Native culture to strengthen the ties between food, history, and communities. Nephi Craig, a chef of Apache and Navajo heritage, said in a 2016 interview, "Our work with Native foods and Native foodways is really about restoration and of balance, and this reclamation of our identity through food and landscape and health."

Text-Dependent Questions:

1. When the Osage harvest and dry corn the traditional way, how do they know when it's done?
2. What are the basic ingredients of fry bread?
3. How does monoculture harm traditional ways of eating?

Research Project:

Native Americans named months according to an important event or symbol of that month, such as "wolf" or "strawberry." Make a calendar with descriptions of the months, and plot out some of the Native ceremonies and festivals and when they happened.

BIG MEALS

Part of the way modern Native American chefs are trying to reconnect people today with the past is by looking at the healthy ways Native Americans used to eat. Some of them revolve around the main parts of meals.

Indigenous people depended on the skills of hunters to bring in wild game, both large and small. The flavors and textures of bison, moose, elk, deer (right), rabbits, squirrels, turkey, and duck were just a few of the choices. Some animals, like lizards or frogs, fell under "foraging" and were collected by women and children. A basic stew recipe with tomatoes, root vegetables, and onions served equally well whether the meat was fresh venison or dried buffalo jerky softened through cooking.

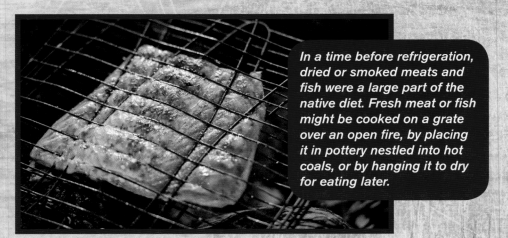

In a time before refrigeration, dried or smoked meats and fish were a large part of the native diet. Fresh meat or fish might be cooked on a grate over an open fire, by placing it in pottery nestled into hot coals, or by hanging it to dry for eating later.

Corn also proved useful not as just a food, but as a vessel for cooking. Corn shucks were like the Native answer to aluminum foil. They could wrap it around meat or vegetables as they were being cooked, holding moisture in the food so that it cooked thoroughly without drying out or burning.

Tamales, for example, now a staple of Mexican cooking, can trace their beginnings to Native Americans who lived in current-day Mexico and the southwestern United States.

Seafood was popular throughout the Americas, from whole salmon steaks grilled on a hot stone or smoked, to diced fish mixed with onions, tomatoes, hot peppers, and avocados, and doused in lemon and lime juice to make ceviche. Shellfish, including mussels, clams, crabs, and shrimp were steamed and flavored with ingredients from the environment they came from: seaweed and saltwater.

Whether turkey was on the table at the first Thanksgiving is debatable. What is known is that wild turkey was part of the indigenous diet, along with goose, quail, and other fowl. Although modern instructions caution to cook meat thoroughly, indigenous people recognized that the breasts (white meat) of birds like squab and duck were tastier and more tender when cooked rare. The cavity of the bird, between the legs and breast, was stuffed with vegetables and seasonings that released moisture and flavor during the cooking process—a technique still used today.

No one knows who "invented" soups and stews. They've been around virtually as long as people have. Every culture has put their mark on the classic one-pot meal, though. Today, the northeastern United States is famous for its seafood chowders. Originally, Natives used a type of clam called quahogs, combined with corn, beans, tomatoes, and a clear broth to make their chowders. Over time, Europeans changed the recipe, adding fish or other seafood, switching out corn for potatoes, and thickening the broth with milk or cream that came from cattle imported from Europe.

Succotash—from a Wampanoag word meaning "boiled corn kernels"—is another basic dish shared by many Native American tribes. It starts with a blend of corn and beans, two ingredients available throughout the whole of the Americas in different varieties. Lima beans that were native to Peru, or cranberry beans from Colombia, worked equally well in this versatile dish. Peppers, onions, tomatoes, and other vegetables and spices were added as available.

4

Moving Forward

Visit any big city in the United States, and it's easy to find restaurants that serve ethnic cuisine, from Mexican to Mediterranean. But restaurants that feature the most American food of all—*Native* American—are almost nonexistent. "We aren't a restaurant culture," explains chef Nephi Craig. "It's still an idea that doesn't match with our core indigenous beliefs." As a result, familiarity with Native American food has traditionally not spread far beyond Native people themselves.

Defining a Cuisine

What *is* Native American food? A third-grader might tell you about the Thanksgiving basics: corn, pumpkins, and cranberries. Ask a Native American chef, and you'll likely get a longer answer, one that includes *wojapi* (chokecherry

Words to Understand

cultural appropriation   taking another's culture and using it as your own

hierarchy   a system or organization in which people or groups are ranked one above the other according to status or authority

50

Combining traditional and more modern ingredients, Native American chefs are trying to merge the old and the new.

sauce) and *wasna* (pemmican), tomatoes and turnips, chilis and chocolate. In fact, it's estimated that about 60 percent of all of the foods eaten in the world today originated in the Americas. Native American food is the foundation of the global diet.

That's a pretty broad definition, though. There are more than 500 different Native tribes in the United States alone, and eating steamed clams in New England is a lot different from eating grilled cactus leaves in New Mexico. At the Smithsonian National Museum of the American Indian in Washington, D.C., the restaurant showcases foods from five different regions in the United States—and even that just scratches the surface.

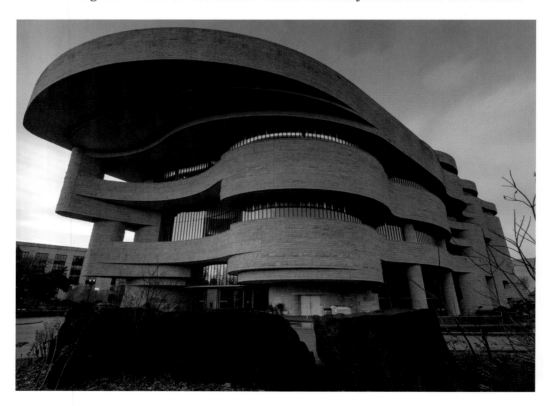

The National Museum of the American Indian is part of the Smithsonian complex in Washington DC. It opened in 2004.

Speaking very generally, Native cuisine has relied on a variety of wild game, birds, and fish, as well as whatever plant foods could be grown or gathered. But time and progress have taken their toll. Wild turnips called *timpsula* once were a staple food among Native Americans. Mothers would send their children to collect them, describing how one plant's branches "pointed" to the next plant, making them easier to find. Now, these prairie turnips have become somewhat rare, possibly because their preferred habitat—virgin prairie—has been converted to farmland.

Individual recipes or cooking methods have vanished as the thread of the oral tradition has broken. The details of how to forage, harvest, and use certain foods were largely passed down through word of mouth, and some of it has been lost forever. Chef Sean Sherman has done a lot of detailed detective work trying to discover the old ways of doing things—including reading written works, and talking to people to mine their memories. He's learned old techniques for drying meat and grinding corn, and age-old tricks for harvesting herbs in the wild. In the kitchen, he's tried various ways of doing things to see what works best. And when there's no information to be had? He relies on his own creativity, just as his ancestors likely would have.

Sherman said in a 2016 interview, "Canada shouldn't be defined by *poutine* [French fries with gravy], and America shouldn't be defined by hamburgers and Coca-Cola. There's nothing wrong with those pieces, but there's so much history and culture behind our landscape and our regions."

Some Native Americans feel that the lesser status historically given to their cultures shows up in the attitude toward their food. Freddie Bitsoie, the head chef at the Smithsonian National Museum of the American Indian, said in a 2017 interview, "What is eaten is based on where the culture stands, and it happens to be that most of Native culture, along with other ethnic cultures, are at the bottom of the food **hierarchy**."

That's changing, though. Lois Ellen Frank, who is of Kiowa descent, studies Native American food. In a 2016 interview, she said, "I think people now want to know the story and eat the story, and the story is that there are very rich and delicious native foods."

New Approaches

Not only did reservation life prevent Native Americans from living in the ways they were used to, it also made it difficult to earn a living. Even today, the rates of unemployment and poverty on reservations are extremely high. But there are efforts to both combat economic hardship and reestablish traditional foodways.

The idea of food sovereignty means that people have control over what they eat, with access to food that is healthy and part of their culture. Across

Revitalizing Native American cuisine

A Meal of Memories

Chef Nephi Craig has a lot on his plate. He focuses on making dishes that represent his Native cuisine, and serving them in a way that honors his heritage. For one meal, he chooses the grain amaranth, because it's a symbol of defying colonial oppression. (The Spanish conquistador Hernan Cortes forbade Natives to cultivate this food, which was sacred to them.) Craig also selects butternut squash, which holds its seeds inside and represents the ability to sustain a civilization in the face of adversity.

Next, Craig places the ingredients on the plate in a particular arrangement that tells a story. The upper right quadrant corresponds to *Nitsáhakees*, the Navajo concept of thoughts and ideas. Moving clockwise, the next quadrant is *Nahat'á*, where something is in the planning stage. Both of these parts of the plate are empty, as nothing is yet tangible. The third quadrant, *Iiná*, is the execution of the plan, and the fourth, *Sihasin*, is the result. Here, the food is presented and the meal takes shape. Says Craig, "The ultimate goal of the dish is to activate ancestral knowledge and create a powerful taste experience."

the United States, many Native Americans are working toward this idea. It might be as simple as planting a community garden, or as ambitious as creating a company that manufactures and sells Native foods.

Chef Sean Sherman now calls himself the Sioux chef. (That's a pun. Sioux is pronounced the same as the French word *sous*, which means "under." In French, a sous chef is an assistant to the main chef.) He has taken the lead in efforts to promote Native American cuisine, forming a group called North American Traditional Indigenous Food Systems (NATIFS). Its purpose is to educate Native Americans about traditional foodways, help them start businesses, and grow rare Native foods that have almost disappeared. Sherman hopes this will help Native American communities, as well as educate non-Natives. "When you want to learn people's culture, it's so much easier to approach it through food," he said in a 2017 interview.

Old and New

Although there's a lot of talk about returning to Native, indigenous foods, the reality is that it's impossible to entirely go back to an earlier lifestyle. Instead, the resurgence in Native cooking recognizes the best of the old—traditional ingredients and techniques—and pairs it with the best of the new.

Freddie Bitsoie says, "It drives me crazy when people say, 'This isn't Native enough' or 'This is too Native.' When people put a gauge on culture, it is very divisive. Food was never meant to divide people.... Foods become extinct, something better comes along, something more efficient. Something will always change," he says. "If you are safe and do everything from the past, you are just going to be a boring one-hit wonder."

Energy Efficient

In the Lakota language, "tanka" translates to "live life powerfully." And a company based on the Pine Ridge Indian Reservation in South Dakota has wrapped that power into the Tanka energy bar, which combines the traditional foods of buffalo meat and cranberries. The bars are packed with protein—but no artificial preservatives, since those weren't available to Native Americans. Mark Tilsen, one of the inventors of the Tanka bar, credits "some grandma thousands of years ago" for discovering that when meat is mixed with fruit, it creates its own preservative. The company's mission is to produce an authentic, healthy food for Native Americans (and anyone else who wants to eat it); reintroduce buffalo to their native lands; and create an industry that will help the reservation economically.

However, in promoting indigenous foods and diets, some Native Americans worry that it could erode or distort their culture. When non-Native cooks prepare Native foods and present them as their own creations, Sherman says the result is **cultural appropriation**—taking another's culture and using it as their own. Others disagree. Lois Ellen Frank says, "The truth is, we've been sharing recipes for millennia. How is someone else cooking a rack of venison and using a chokecherry reduction appropriation? If that encouraged them to buy their wild rice from a Native organization, I've succeeded."

New generations of Native Americans will strive to continue to preserve their ancient traditions through the stresses of modern living.

Ultimately, Native cultures are not one people but many. Their perspectives will differ, just as their foodways do, but many share the goal of renewing and expressing their cultural identity through food. Historically, Native peoples have suffered during some times and flourished during others, but through it all, they have held onto ancient traditions even as they have found new ways forward. The story of Native food is one that reflects the journey of the people themselves.

Text-Dependent Questions:

1. Approximately what percent of the world's foods originated in the Americas?

2. How did parents help their children find prairie turnips?

3. What is one goal of the company that makes Tanka bars?

Research Project:

Preserving heirloom seeds and cultivating new plants is an important part of renewing indigenous foodways. Look for plants that are native to your area, but have become scarce. Are there any you could grow?

DESSERT

Although most Americans today equate sweet desserts with white sugar, that substance was unknown in the Americas until the arrival of Europeans. Instead, Native Americans used fruit, and—most famously—tree sap to satisfy their cravings for something sweet.

Almost everyone is familiar with maple syrup, made by tapping the sap of a number of varieties of maple trees and then boiling it until it turns into a thick syrup. The sugar maple makes the sweetest (and most plentiful) syrup, but other maple species also work. Maples aren't the only option; birch, walnut, and sycamore trees also produce sap with distinctive flavors. Native Americans used the syrup as a dipping sauce for cornbread or fruit; it could also be boiled down even further until it hardened into a sugary candy.

Fruit was another common source of sugar. Apples, apricots, grapes, and berries were indigenous to the Americas. Fruit could be eaten raw or cooked; wojapi was a berry sauce that was as basic as combining fruit and water and cooking it until it thickened into the consistency of jam. If they wanted it sweeter, a dollop of syrup did the trick. Native Americans stretched summer and autumn harvests into winter by drying fruit in the sun or on heated stones. Fruit could be dried whole, or mashed into a puree, rolled out, and then cooked into fruit leathers.

Of course, refrigeration was unknown before the 20th century, but Native Americans who lived in colder climates sometimes enjoyed an ancient form of ice cream. In Alaska, the Inupiaq tribe made a treat called akutaq by whipping together an assortment of berries with fish oil and snow. Even surrounded by a natural freezer, the result did not last for long!

Find Out More

Books

Berzok, Linda Murray. *American Indian Food.* New York: Greenwood, 2005.

Carew-Miller, Anna. *Native American Cooking.* Broomall, PA: Mason Crest, 2013.

Divina, Fernando and Marlene Divina, with the Smithsonian National Museum of the American Indian. *Foods of the Americas: Native Recipes and Traditions.* Berkeley, CA: Ten Speed Press, 2010.

Mann, Charles C. *Before Columbus: The Americas of 1491.* New York: Holt McDougal, 2009.

Small, Cathleen. *Colonial Interactions with Native Americans.* New York: Cavendish Square, 2018.

Websites

http://www.nativeland.org/native-foodways/
Check out some efforts to preserve Native foodways and listen to first-person oral histories by Native Americans from various regions.

https://www.southernfoodways.org/tag/native-american/Several stories explore the role of Native American food in the southern United States.

https://foodwaysproject.com/2015/11/03/celebrating-indigenous-food-ways-for-native-american-heritage-month/
This website features a collection of articles and videos about food sovereignty and reviving Native American foodways.

Series Glossary of Key Terms

acclimate to get used to something

assimilate become part of a different society, country, or group

bigotry treating the members of a racial or ethnic group with hatred and intolerance

culinary having to do with the preparing of food

diaspora a group of people who live outside the area in which they had lived for a long time or in which their ancestors lived

emigrate leave one's home country to live in another country

exodus a mass departure of people from one place to another

first-generation American someone born in the United States whose parents were foreign born

immigrants those who enter another country intending to stay permanently

naturalize to gain citizenship, with all its rights and privileges

oppression a system of forcing people to follow rules or a system that restricts freedoms

presentation in this series, the style in which food is plated and served

Index

Photo Credits

Author Bio

Diane Bailey has written more than 50 nonfiction books for kids and teens, on topics ranging from science to sports to celebrities. She also works as a freelance editor, helping authors who write novels for children and young adults. Diane has two sons and two dogs, and lives in Kansas.